OHIO

A PHOTOGRAPHIC CELEBRATION

FOREWORD BY RICHARD F. CELESTE

AMERICAN & WORLD GEOGRAPHIC PUBLISHING

JOHN L. RANDOLPH

HEIDI WELLER

Above: *Holmes County harvest.*
Right: *A black-eyed Susan perch for a passing grasshopper.*
Facing page: *Toledo's Portside Festival Market Place.*

Title page: *Cardinal, Ohio's state bird, amidst dogwood blossoms.* MASLOWSKI PHOTO

Front cover: *Cincinnati.* TOM DIETRICH

Back cover, top: *In Huron County.*
BARBARA DURHAM
Bottom: *Sunset from Marblehead on Lake Erie.*
TOM TILL

ISBN 0-938314-98-X

Foreword © 1991 Richard F. Celeste
© 1991 American & World Geographic Publishing,
P.O. Box 5630, Helena, MT 59604. (406) 443-2842
Printed in Hong Kong

ABOUT
THE
AUTHOR

A native Ohioan, born in Cleveland, Richard F. Celeste served as his state's 64th governor from 1982 to 1990. He also was elected to the Ohio House of Representatives for two terms representing his hometown district, and as Lieutenant Governor for one term. Interests ranging from education reform to economic development have marked his public career. He lived in Great Britain as a Rhodes Scholar and in India as a foreign service officer, and traveled widely as Peace Corps Director (1978-1980)—but he always came home to Ohio.

Foreword

What is round on both ends and high in the middle? OHIO is the answer to that youthful brain teaser. The name is rooted in the Iroquois word "O-he-yo" meaning "great river" given to that forested and fertile land which stretches from the banks of the Ohio River north to the shores of Lake Erie, where the Marblehead Lighthouse has for generations beamed both a welcome as well as a warning.

Ohio is the quintessential American state, carved out of the wilderness in the late eighteenth century by settlers from New England headed toward the Connecticut Western Reserve and adventurers rafting down the Ohio River staking out new lives in the Northwest Territory. By the early nineteenth century, more than a million passengers a year took flat bottoms and paddle wheelers down the great river past Marietta, the territory's first settlement (named after Marie Antoinette), heading west perhaps toward Cincinnati or beyond.

Louis Bromfield, Pulitzer Prize–winning novelist who was born near Mansfield and lived in France and India before returning to his beloved Malabar Farm, once described Ohio as "the furthest East of the West and the furthest West of the East, the furthest North of the South and the furthest South of the North" in the United States. Senator John Glenn is fond of saying that "if you squeezed the United States into one space, you would have the State of Ohio."

Today Ohio's license plates assert proudly: "The Heart of It All." Within overnight delivery of two thirds of the nation's population and sixty percent of its manufacturing; at the near point between the Great Lakes watershed; on the doorstep of the Great Plains and the westward expansion; the freedom station on the underground railroad—Ohioans feel comfortable in our claim. Today Malabar Farm is a state park facility, still operated in accordance with the conservation practices that farmer Louis Bromfield fiercely advocated and offering tours of the "big house" in which celebrity Bromfield welcomed equally celebrated guests. Here in 1945, neighbors recall, Humphrey Bogart and Lauren Bacall were married.

HEIDI WELLER

Above: Primitive sugaring off of maple syrup at Malabar Farm.

Ohio's rich history is closely woven with its geography. The Lake Erie islands provided shelter for young Commodore Oliver Hazard Perry's ragtag array of ships on the eve of his upstart victory over the British naval forces in 1813. "We have met the enemy and they are ours—two ships, two brigs, one schooner, and one sloop," Perry reported to General William Henry Harrison. In southern Ohio, the 1,245-foot-long Great Serpent Mound, an Indian burial mound, hugs the earth in silent witness of still earlier Ohio residents.

Ohio joined the Union in 1803, the seventeenth state and the first to achieve statehood under the terms of the Northwest Ordinance. That remarkable document, the finest legacy of the Article of Confederation that preceded

Marblehead Lighthouse on Lake Erie.

President Ulysses S. Grant's birthplace, Point Pleasant.

our Constitution, thus guaranteed that Ohio would be a pioneer in public education and a hotbed of abolitionist sentiment. It is no accident that William Holmes McGuffey, who helped ensure the literacy of several generations of Americans, produced his remarkable "Readers" at Miami University in Oxford, one of the first institutions of higher education (along with Ohio University in Athens) to be created in the Northwest Territory.

More than 130 institutions of higher education bring distinction to the state. Oberlin pioneered in coeducation; Antioch in work-study, Wilberforce University is the oldest historically black college north of the Mason-Dixon line; Ohio State is the largest single-site campus in the country.

AGRICULTURE HAS BEEN historically—and with food processing and marketing is still—the number one industry in Ohio. Small wonder that a plaque in the State House Rotunda commemorates A.B. Graham, founding father of 4-H. Ohio leads the nation in making Swiss cheese, exports soybeans to Japan and Korea, produces outstanding dairy cattle. Family farms still dominate Ohio agriculture, and on the back roads of Knox and Holmes counties, you can spot Amish farmers working with horsedrawn plows.

Ohioans love hard work, whether in the field or in the factory—and to-

Soybeans in northeastern Ohio.

day, more and more in the office, laboratory, or shop. The dream of work in America brought generations of German farmers to Ohio's rural villages and towns in the latter part of the 1800s. The straight lines that divide one western county from another often divided German Lutherans from German Catholics. That same dream of work brought generations of Italian, Polish, Czech, and other European immigrants to work in the steel mills of Youngstown and the machine tool plants in Cleveland, to build ships in Lorain, and to assemble autos in Toledo. Ohio's cities became the capitals of burgeoning industries— from rubber in Akron (home also of the Soap Box Derby and birthplace of Al- coholics Anonymous) to glass in Toledo (remembered by many, too, for Tony Packo's famous Hungarian sausage sandwiches celebrated by Toledoan Jamie Farr on television's M*A*S*H.

    Many of the inventions of the Industrial Revolution were nurtured by

Buckeye entrepreneurs—Thomas Edison, Harvey Firestone, Charles Kettering, and, of course, our most famous bicycle-tinkers, Wilbur and Orville Wright. Ohioans feel that it is only right and proper that the state whose sons were first in flight is also the state whose sons were first in space—John Glenn, in earth orbit, and Neil Armstrong, stepping onto the moon. Each year thousands of visitors celebrate this legacy at the Air Force Museum at Wright-Patterson Air Force Base near Dayton.

JUST AS TIME has brought dramatic changes to flight since the days of the Wright Brothers, so, too, Ohio's cities have undergone dramatic change. Proctor and Gamble still anchors Cincinnati, but from beautiful new twin towers designed by Kohn, Pedersen, and Fox in 1985. And downtown Cincinnati has become one of the most inviting in the nation, with overhead walkways knitting together famous retailers and first-class hotels with the beautiful Fountain Square and ever-active convention center. Dayton is not only home to NCR (once National Cash Register) but also the creator of Lexus and Nexus, Mead Data. In Youngstown, steel mills are virtually silenced but the city's heritage is recalled at a breath-taking museum designed by Michael Graves.

Cleveland is still the center of Ohio's largest metropolitan area, although Columbus has outgrown the northern city proper. While manufacturing remains the cornerstone of the economy in northeastern Ohio, it is now characterized by some of the most sophisticated technologies in the world. From polymers to sensors—Cleveland has won national recognition and investment. Today Lake Erie is clean and, on any sunny summer day, dotted with sailboats and fishing charters. The landmark Terminal Tower on Public Square boasts one of the most exciting new downtown malls in the United States—called On the Avenue—and nearby, the Flats, along the Cuyahoga River, is home to a remarkable array of crowded nightspots.

Columbus, which became the state capital only after two other communities—Chillicothe and Zanesville—served briefly, has grown from small town to sophisticated city.

The nation's most avant garde artists now look forward to performing or exhibiting at the Wexner Center for the Arts on the Ohio State Campus. Enterprises like Battelle Memorial Institute, the OnLine Computer Library Center, and Chemical Abstracts enjoy national and international reputations which

Above: Hopkins water mill north of Youngstown.

Facing page: Proctor and Gamble headquarters, Cincinnati.

Trumbull County Courthouse, Warren.

bring visitors to central Ohio from around the world. Moreover, as Honda has built its second assembly plant just 45 minutes from downtown Columbus, the workplace here—like those of many other Ohio communities—has taken on an increasingly mulitcultural character.

Ironically, Ohio's small communities, not its cities, have been the magnets drawing many foreign visitors—and investors. Small town life shapes the tone and temperament of most Ohioans. Ohio's small towns have inspired novels from Sherwood Anderson's *Winesburg, Ohio,* to Helen Santmeyer's recent prize-winning epic, *And Ladies of the Club.* They have produced a diverse cast of characters from Annie Oakley to Clark Gable, from James Thurber to

Toni Morrison. However one views it, the best small town values have had a profound influence on the character of Ohioans.

Hard work is one important part of that character. So is our commitment to faith and family. Not surprisingly, Ohio is dotted with the names of Utopian communities—from Mt. Hope to New Concord. Shaker Heights honors its founders in name. Joseph Smith set forth from Kirtland on the journey that took him eventually to Salt Lake City.

Methodist churches are a predictable landmark in virtually every community in Ohio, and just down the highway from the Methodist Theological School in Delaware, Ohio, is the Josephium, the only Pontifical Seminary in

Sheep shearing occupies these Wyandot County farmers during the late-winter months.

the United States. One must journey to Cincinnati to find Hebrew Union Seminary, the first Jewish institution of higher learning in the United States (founded in 1875).

To hard work and faith, Ohioans add family. Ohioans divorce less frequently than most Americans; Ohioans move less frequently as well. We are homebodies. When we venture out, it is for fun—to enjoy nature and sport.

We hike the Buckeye Trails. We visit Old Man's Cave. We fish in Lake Erie or a farm pond. Ohioans hold 1,201,755 fishing permits, and 771,091 hunting permits, and license 378,249 boats. We camp by the glacial grooves on Kelleys Island; we bicycle through the Cuyahoga Natural Area; we count covered bridges; we visit county fairs. Do we ever visit county fairs! From the Tomato Festival in Reynoldsburg to the Balloon Festival in Marysville to the Pumpkin Show in Circleville, where you can eat pumpkin ten different ways, Ohio counts more than 100 county fairs and festivals each year. The granddaddy for fairgoers, however, is the Ohio State Fair, which takes place for seventeen days each August at the Fairgrounds in the capital city. In 1990, the Ohio State Fair even outdrew that of Texas to stake a claim as the largest (and many would say, the best) state fair anywhere in the United States. From

RAY MATOUSEK

4-H to fine arts; fair food to tractor pulls; 975 classes of horses and 238 classes of pigs to llamas and rabbits and seventy-pound squash; from midway rides to grandstand entertainment like Willie Nelson and New Kids on the Block, the Ohio State Fair offers the best six-dollar bargain in the state.

Family and fun are also part of Ohioans' love of sport and competition. On Fridays, most Ohioans can be found at a high school football or basketball game. In Massillon—a few miles from the NFL Football Hall of Fame—every boy baby is given a football by the school boosters' club. Northern Ohioans tend to cheer for the Browns and the Indians (and dream of pennant races in years gone by). South of U.S. Interstate 70, folks root for the Bengals and the Reds (and relish the four-game sweep that made the latter World Champions in 1990). In Columbus, caught in the middle, professional sports loyalties are divided. But on each fall Saturday afternoon, Ohioans unite to cheer on the Ohio State football team—treating the Buckeyes like the one thing better than a professional sports franchise.

Ohioans cherish our rich natural heritage. And we cherish, too, our contributions to our nation's history, whether that means the seven Presidents we claims as our own, or Victoria Woodhull—the first woman to run for President (in 1872).

Above: Lake fish for dinner tonight!

Facing page, *top: On the midway at Cedar Point, Sandusky.*
Bottom: The Buckeye State took its nickname from the fruit of the horse chestnut tree.

Above: Flag girls take time for a last-minute huddle before performing at the Circleville Pumpkin Show.

Facing page: *Cedar Falls in its namesake state park in the Hocking Hills offers cool respite on a muggy summer afternoon.*

WE ALL CHERISH THE VALUES that have shaped our common life—hard work and faith, family and fun. And we welcome visitors to our special place. We want folks to feel at home. When American Electric Power moved its headquarters from New York City to Columbus, some of its executives balked at the thought of leaving civilization behind. Chairman and CEO "Pete" White reports, "We found everything we were afraid of leaving…clearly hidden right here." Within a short time the skeptical executives became enthusiastic Buckeye boosters.

More than one young person, hitch-hiking along the Interstate, has had the experience of being taken home to a modest frame house in a village or town for a home-cooked meal before being taken back to the highway for the continuing journey.

In the best sense, we *are* middle America. Here we turn Vienna into "Veye-enna" and Russia into "Roo-she"—and the out-of-towner is quickly spotted. A few years ago, when a news magazine wanted to profile an American community, the editors chose Springfield. In that same year's Presidential election, a TV network wanted a typical American voter; their choice—a Dayton housewife. Why, you can even still get a five-cent cup of coffee at McCarthy Pharmacy in Marysville!

Finally, to be an Ohioan is to cherish the four seasons that help us mark the passing of time—fresh and new in the spring, full and flowering in the summer, crisp and colorful in the fall, then cold and quiet in the winter. These seasons lead us from youth to age, from one generation to the next. When we travel to a distinct place, a different climate, we find ourselves drawn home by the seasons—to smell the fresh breeze with the promise of rain and daffodils in the spring; to taste summer's sweet corn and lake perch; to see the colorful leaves and the high school marching bands in the autumn; and to feel winter's deep freeze and promise of thaw to come.

Regardless of season or storm, the Marblehead lighthouse, solid and solitary, guides travelers safely home—home to Ohio.

Above: Upper Sandusky and the Wyandot County Courthouse from the air.
Left: Although built in the 1930s, Wildwood Manor House and its furnishings reproduce Georgian England. Today the home and its 460 acres of parkland are part of Toledo's city park system.

Facing page: The Green River, Sandusky Bay wetlands.

Along the Maumee riverfront in downtown Toledo.

Above: *Footprints of great glaciers on Kelleys Island.*

Facing page: *Jack-o-lanterns vine-ripen near Toledo.*

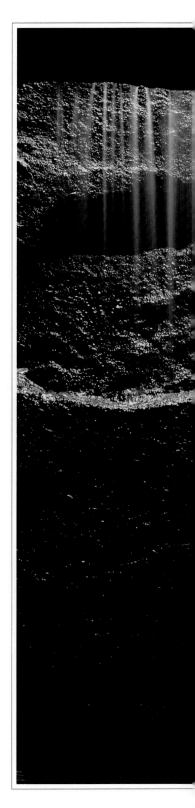

Above: *The first human to step onto the moon, Neil Armstrong, is honored with a museum at his hometown of Wapakoneta, where his Gemini 8 capsule is on exhibit.*
Right: *A vast sandstone formation is protected at Nelson Kennedy Ledges State Park near Garrettsville.*

DENNIS BARNES

Above: Moonrise over Cleveland, with the landmark Terminal Tower at right.
Left: Tower City Center Mall, in Cleveland's Terminal Tower.
Right: Going for the lead at Thistledown race track, North Randall.

BARBARA DURHAM PHOTOS RIGHT & ABOVE

Above: *Portrait of summertime patience.*
Right: *Findley Lake near Wellington offers peaceful swimming, camping and fishing an hour away from Cleveland.*

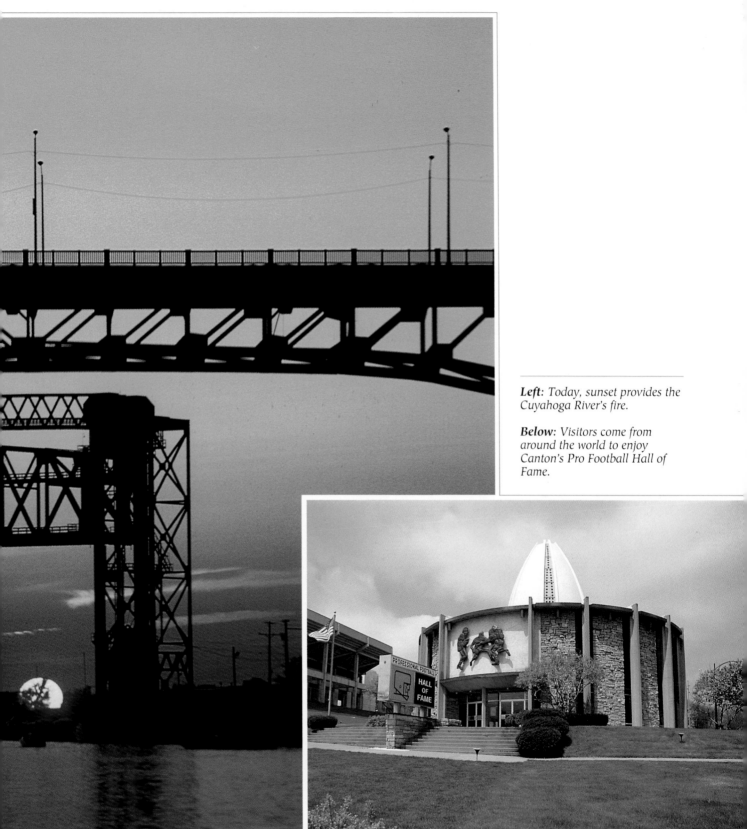

Left: *Today, sunset provides the Cuyahoga River's fire.*

Below: *Visitors come from around the world to enjoy Canton's Pro Football Hall of Fame.*

JUSTINE HILL

Above: Fairport Harbor, Mentor Headlands State Park.
Right: At the Great Lakes Historical Museum, overlooking Lake Erie in Vermilion.

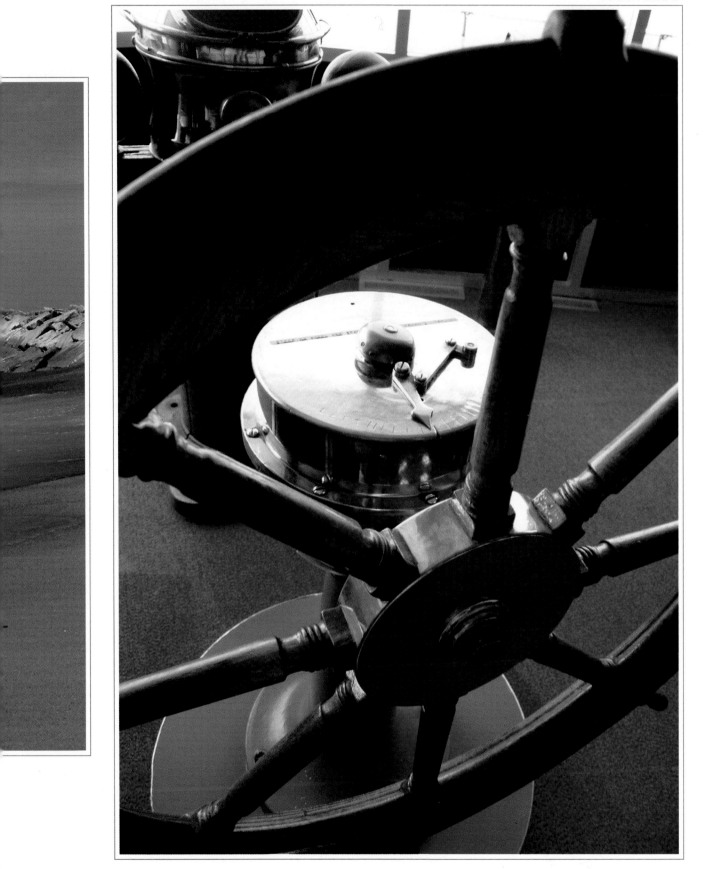

Above: In downtown Akron, 36 silos formerly used by Quaker Oats house the Quaker Square Hotel and Convention Center.

Right: Honoring the assassinated 25th President, William McKinley, in Niles, where he was born in 1843.

Facing page: Springtime in Rhododendron Allée at Stan Hywet Hall and Gardens, Akron. Once the estate of Goodyear Tire and Rubber co-founder Frank Seiberling, today Stan Hywet is open to the public.

BARBARA DURHAM

Above: Classic barn red on a Burton-area Amish farm.
Right: An Amish family near Middlefield.

Facing page: Lehman Hardware, Kidron, serves the needs of both Amish and "English" (non-Amish) Wayne County customers.

Right: Harvesting lettuce in a climate-controlled bubble at Pretzer Farms, Wooster.
Below: River fishing on a humid day.

Above: *Of a spring day, Mama Mallard and her new family take the air.*
Left: *A white-tailed fawn.*

Above: Historic preservation is alive and hearty on East Washington Street, Medina.
Right: In Youngstown's Mill Creek Park, Ford Nature Center—once a private residence—shows the New England influence on eastern Ohio.

Facing page: It is always 54 degrees for the stalactites and stalagmites—and visitors—inside Ohio Caverns near West Liberty.

Above: Once a "station" on the Underground Railroad, this house remembers the days when crossing the Ohio River promised freedom for escaping slaves.
Right: Spring rains run off over the sandstone ledges of Old Man's Cave State Park in the Hocking Hills.

*An abandoned iron furnace in Vinton County **(right)** and a deserted coal mine in Jackson County **(below)** speak of early-day industries in Ohio's least-populous area.*

***Facing page:** Bucyrus's Picking and Company produces fine copperware by hand, still using 19th-century techniques.*

HEIDI WELLER PHOTOS ABOVE AND BELOW

Flourishing downtown Cincinnati:
Above: *Dusk falls on Fountain Square.*
Right: *Skyline rising above the Ohio River.*

Southern Ohioans fill Riverfront Stadium **(above)** on the Ohio River in Cincinnati to cheer baseball's Reds **(right)** and football's Bengals. **(facing page, top)**.

Facing page: But northern Ohioans give their loyalties to Cleveland's Indians (Sandy Alomar at bat, **left**) and Browns.

COURTESY CINCINNATI BENGALS

DAVID LIAM KYLE PHOTO COURTESY CLEVELAND INDIANS

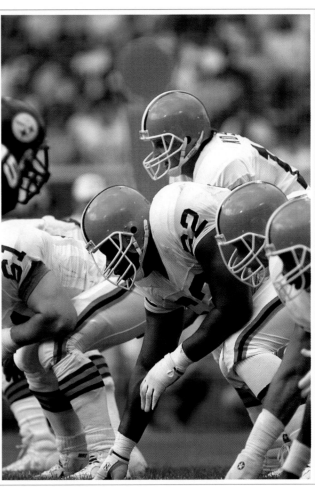

COURTESY CLEVELAND BROWNS

Above: *A World War II-vintage B-29 Superfortress bomber on exhibit at the U.S. Air Force Museum, Dayton.*

Facing page: *Fresh from the farmer's market—in downtown Dayton.*

Downtown Dayton and the Great Miami River—historically both servant and scourge.

Above: *Seriously enjoying the annual festival at Cuyahoga Valley National Recreation Area, Cleveland.*

Facing page: *Nature's artistry at sunset in Big Run park, Columbus.*

Autumn touches Vinton County.

BARBARA DURHAM

Above: *This nighttime hockey game is doubly lighted.*

Facing page: *The port of Huron grew where the Huron River meets Lake Erie.*

Above and right: *A covered bridge and rolling farmland on Clear Creek Road, Fairfield County.*

Facing page: *Sure sign of spring.*

A bower of autumn color along Seldom Seen Road near Powell.

The Hopewell Indians' 12-century-old Great Serpent Mound near Locust Grove continues to intrigue visitors.

Left and below: *Author-agriculturist Louis Bromfield's Malabar Farm in Richland County is open to the public.*

Facing page: *The Orangery of Mansfield's Kingwood Center, once a private estate and now a public arts center and nature-horticulture preserve.*

HEIDI WELLER PHOTOS ABOVE AND BELOW

DENNIS BARNES

Above: Making friends—cautiously.
Right: Up, up, and away over Marysville.

Above: *The heart of the matter at the annual Circleville Pumpkin Show.*

Facing page: *Early autumn graces the campus of Ohio Wesleyan University, Delaware.*

The Scioto River and downtown
Columbus—now the state's
largest metropolitan area as
well as its capital.

Above: *Old architecture meets new in Columbus.*

Facing page: *Capitol Square, Columbus.*

Above: *The Ohio State Capitol,*
completed in 1861, is one of the nation's
best examples of Doric Greek Revival
architecture.
Facing page: *The Great Seal of the State*
of Ohio in the capitol's rotunda dome.

Above: *Ohio Center Mall, downtown Columbus.*

Facing page: *Columbus's Franklin Park conservatory, 12,500 square feet under glass, was built in 1859.*

JAMES FRANK

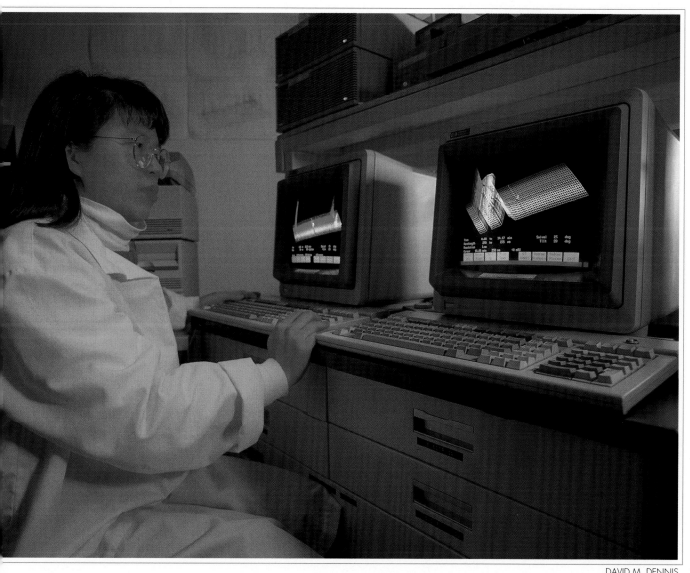

Above: *Gas chromatograph in the Biotechnology Center at Ohio State University.*

Facing page: *University Hall, Ohio State University, Columbus.*

Above: *Enjoying autumn in a Cleveland city park.*

Facing page: *Swans are popular features, and year-round residents, of many city parks around the state.*

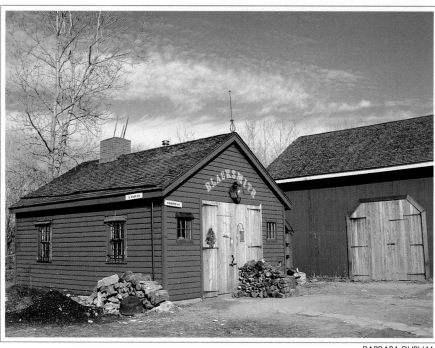

Costumed interpreters add to the ambiance of the reconstructed 19th-century Ohio Village at the Ohio Historical Center, Columbus.

Above: *Riverdale Road Bridge over the Grand River in Ashtabula County, built in 1874, was restored in 1981.*

Facing page: *Harvesttime still life.*

Above: *New England aster.*
Left: *Vast beds of hundreds of tulip varieties are a springtime tradition at Kingwood Center, Mansfield.*

Above: *A bridge built by the New York Central Railroad near Nevada in Wyandot County now serves Amtrak.*
Left: *The delicate touch-me-not.*

Facing page: *The Ohio River Museum at Marietta.*

Above and right: Fresh-picked roasting ears and sliced tomatoes—basis for many a summer supper—with ripe strawberries for dessert.
Left: Adams County tobacco barns.

Above and right: In Hardin County.

Facing page: After the ice storm.

DENNIS BARNES

Above: *...And this little fellow is just for you.*

Facing page: *Autumn rain down in the valley.*

Overleaf: *Ottawa National Wildlife Refuge, Sandusky Bay.*